BRINGING UP BOYS
BIBLE STUDY
SHAPING THE NEXT GENERATION OF MEN

DR. JAMES DOBSON

developed with Michael O'Neal

LifeWay Press®
Nashville, Tennessee

Published by LifeWay Press®
Copyright © 2014 by Siggie, LLC

Bringing Up Boys © 2014 by Dr. James Dobson. Published by Tyndale House Publishers;
Carol Stream, IL. Used by Permission.

ISBN: 978-1-4158-7805-7
Item: 005558790

Dewey decimal classification: 649
Subject headings: CHILD REARING \ BOYS \ MEN

Unless indicated otherwise, all Scripture quotations are taken from the Holman Christian Standard Bible.
Copyright © 1999, 2000, 2002, 2003, 2009 by Holman Bible Publishers. Used by permission. Holman
Christian Standard Bible® and HCSB® are federally registered trademarks of Holman Bible Publishers.
Scripture marked NKJV are from the New King James Version. Copyright © 1979, 1980, 1982, Thomas
Nelson, Inc., Publishers.

To order additional copies of this resource, write to LifeWay Church Resources, Customer Service,
One LifeWay Plaza, Nashville, TN 37234-0113; fax 615.251.5933; phone 800.458.2772; order online
at *www.lifeway.com* or email *orderentry@lifeway.com;* or visit the LifeWay Christian Store serving you.

Printed in the United States of America

Adult Ministry Publishing, LifeWay Church Resources, One LifeWay Plaza, Nashville, TN 37234-0152

Contents

About the Author

DR. JAMES DOBSON is the founder and president of Family Talk, a non-profit organization that produces his radio program, "Dr. James Dobson's Family Talk." He is the author of more than 50 books dedicated to the preservation of the family, including *The New Dare to Discipline; Love for a Lifetime; Life on the Edge; Love Must Be Tough; The New Strong-Willed Child; When God Doesn't Make Sense; Bringing Up Boys; Bringing Up Girls; Head Over Heels;* and, most recently, *Dr. Dobson's Handbook of Family Advice.*

Dr. Dobson served as an associate clinical professor of pediatrics at the University of Southern California School of Medicine for fourteen years and on the attending staff of Children's Hospital of Los Angeles for seventeen years in the divisions of Child Development and Medical Genetics. He has been active in governmental affairs and has advised three U.S. presidents on family matters.

He earned his PhD from the University of Southern California (1967) in child development and holds eighteen honorary doctoral degrees. He was inducted in 2009 into the National Radio Hall of Fame.

Dr. Dobson and his wife, Shirley, reside in Colorado Springs, Colorado. They have two grown children, Danae and Ryan, and two grandchildren.

MICHAEL O'NEAL helped with the curriculum development of this study. A pastor in the metro Atlanta area, he has also served as a church planter and professor. Michael and his wife, Carrie, are co-authors of *Just (Stay) Married*, a devotional book that encourages couples to pursue a Christ-centered marriage. Michael and Carrie enjoy life with their two energetic sons, Silas and Hudson.

How to Use This Study

The four sessions of this study may be used weekly or during a weekend retreat. (There's an optional fifth session if your group would like to have a follow-up discussion.) But we recommend that before you dig into this material, you watch the film, *Bringing Up Boys* from the *Dr. James Dobson Presents: Building a Family Legacy* film series. This will lay the groundwork for your study.

This material has been written for a small-group experience, for you and your spouse, or for personal study.

An option to extend or conclude this study is for your group to view the film *Your Legacy* from the *Dr. James Dobson Presents: Building a Family Legacy* film series.

CONNECT: The purpose of the introductory section of each session invites and motivates you to connect with the topic of the session and others in your group.

WATCH: The study DVD contains four DVD clips which include introductions from Ryan Dobson and clips from a talk by Dr. James Dobson, based on the film and the accompanying book *Bringing Up Boys* by Dr. Dobson (Tyndale Momentum; ISBN 978-1-4143-9133-5.)

ENGAGE: This section is the primary focus of each week's group time. You and the other participants will further engage the truths of Scripture and discuss accompanying questions. This section will also include a Wrap Up portion, which concludes the group session and leads to the Reflect section.

REFLECT: This at-home study section helps you dig deeper into Scripture and apply the truths you're learning. Go deeper each week by reading the suggested chapters in the book *Bringing Up Boys* and completing the activities at the end of each session in this study.

Guidelines for Groups

While you can complete this study alone, you will benefit greatly from covering the material with your spouse or with the interaction of a Sunday School class or small group. Here are a few ways to cultivate a valuable experience as you engage in this study.

PREPARATION: To get the most out of each group time, read through the study each week and answer the questions so you're ready to discuss the material. It will also be helpful for you and your group members to have copies of the book *Bringing Up Boys* (ISBN 978-1-4143-9133-5). Read it in advance of the study to prepare, and encourage your members to read the corresponding chapters each week. In your group, don't let one or two people shoulder the entire responsibility for conversation and participation. Everyone can pitch in and contribute.

CONFIDENTIALITY: In the study, you will be prompted to share thoughts, feelings, and personal experiences. Accept others where they are without judgment. Many of the challenges discussed will be private. These should be kept in strict confidence by the group.

RESPECT: Participants must respect each other's thoughts and opinions, providing a safe place for those insights to be shared without fear of judgment or unsolicited advice (including hints, sermons, instructions, and scriptural Band-Aids®). Take off your fix-it hat and leave it at the door, so you can just listen. If advice is requested, then it's OK to lend your opinion, seasoned with grace and offered with love.

ACCOUNTABILITY: Each week, participants will be challenged in their intentional parenting of their sons. Commit to supporting and encouraging each other during the sessions and praying for each other between meetings.

Introduction

From the moment the doctor announced, "It's a boy!"—whether
in a delivery room after nine months of waiting, in an ultrasound
room after twenty weeks of curiosity, or after receiving the news of a
successful adoption—you have been dreaming, hoping, and praying
about your son.

While you may wonder if he will become a political leader, an artist, a
techie, a scientist, a doctor, a professional athlete, a missionary, or a
dad, ultimately, your greatest desire as a Christian parent is that your
son would grow to be a man after God's own heart.

Your son will be bombarded by our culture that promotes the world's
agenda, enticing him with values that are not God honoring. You must
intentionally teach him from God's Word, cultivating an environment
in your home that encourages him to grow in godly character.

The aim of this study is to motivate and instruct you, a mom or dad,
so that you might lead your son to know that his value and com-
pleteness are in Christ. When you seek the Lord's wisdom as parents,
our Heavenly Father will equip you with what you need as your son
develops into a Christ-honoring man.

While this *Bringing Up Boys Bible Study* experience will not guarantee
that you'll be a perfect parent, it will offer suggestions for creating an
environment for your growth as you participate in a small group with
other parents of boys. Accompanied by a weekly personal "Reflect"
section, guiding you to read the Bible on your own, this study is
designed to suggest questions, to recommend steps to take, and to
share passages from God's Word to inspire and guide you.

As you journey, it's also important to be encouraged by other
parents who have set similar goals for their own sons. The impact
of examining the Scriptures together with other believing parents
is powerful. The Bible calls this experience of brothers and sisters

working together for a common goal, "His body ... the church." And God promises is that when you gather, He will join you. (See Matt. 18:20.) The Holy Spirit will be a member of your group. Around your circle, He will give wisdom. He may speak to you through the others gathered, or He may quietly whisper to you with His "still small voice" (1 Kings 19:12, KJV).

As you engage in this study, my prayer is that God will richly reward your effort and radically bless your family. And may your son's life forever be impacted for good as a result of the time you are investing in this study.

ADVENTURES IN
PARENTING

● **BEFORE YOU BEGIN,** take time to pray as a group. Ask God to teach you how to be a loving parent to your son, just as He is to each of you.

Tell the group a little about yourself (name, kids, and where you grew up).

Describe an adventurous experience in your life.

"Introduce" your son(s) to the group. Tell them a little about him—his activities, what he likes, what he wants to do with his life, and so forth.

Share what you hope to learn from this study and a hope you have for your son(s).

God created boys and girls with distinct differences. Generally speaking, boys are more adventurous, more willing to take risks and to try something dangerous than girls.

When you were a kid, do you remember boys (maybe you?) taking adventurous or dangerous risks? Describe one of them.

WATCH CLIP 1 from the study DVD and answer the following questions:

The clip offered several stories about the daring nature of most boys.

How have you noticed this risk-taking and competitive nature in your son?

What are the long-term benefits of an adventurous nature? What could be the disadvantages?

In what ways could this adventurous spirit create opportunities for your participation in his life?

● **CONTINUE YOUR GROUP TIME** with this discussion guide.

God's Word has sufficient wisdom for you as a parent. As we examine passages of Scripture, consider the following: a) what the words meant to the original audience, b) what they mean to all believers for all time, and c) what the passage means for us today as the parents of sons.

Let's start at the beginning.

● **READ** Genesis 1:2.

If we are created in God's image, we are valuable, we are unique, and we have dignity. When we recognize that others are created in His image, we are compelled to treat them with dignity and value.

> If boys are created in the image of God, and boys tend to be adventurous, what does that reveal to you about God? How does that alter your image of Him? Of your son?

> How does believing that your boy was created to reflect his Creator affect the way you lead and teach him? Would this realization alter the way you talk about him to other parents?

> What are some practical ways you can help your son understand how valuable and precious he is to God?

> How can you help him understand that others are valuable and precious to God too?

OFFERING INSTRUCTION

Although you can't anticipate every choice your son will need to make as he matures, you can promote a receptive environment in your home for wisdom and instruction. Keep in mind that the spirit with which you offer instruction to your son is crucial.

● **READ** Colossians 3:21 and Ephesians 6:4.

What does it mean to "exasperate" our children?

Why are we warned not to "stir up anger" in our kids? What impact can high-spirited anger have on a household?

● **READ** Ephesians 4:29.

In Greek, the word *foul* means *rotten* or *corrupt*.

Discuss how you instruct your son. Consider what rots his spirit and what builds him up. Here's some to get you started:

Instruction that rots	Instruction that builds up
blame	model repentance and
yelling	humility
condescension	forgiveness

Your son needs your wisdom and instruction, and he needs grace. As God's kindness leads us to repentance (see Rom. 2:4), so your kindness can draw him to see his need for a Savior to change his ways.

> Name something your parents said to you (positive or negative) that impacted how you view yourself.

READ Proverbs 15:32.

When you despise yourself, you essentially reject and disconnect yourself. But when you listen to correction, you humble yourself to be open to change.

> How can you present this verse to your son, helping him see how to value (not despise) himself in accepting instruction?

> Consider the goal of your instruction: Is it to get good behavior or to raise a boy with a heart that asks what would be pleasing to the Lord? Why?

THIS WEEK'S INSIGHTS

• • •

- Boys are made in the image of our adventurous God.
- Boys need instruction that builds them up according to their needs.
- Our goal as parents is to give our sons a lifelong passion for following Christ, not simply high marks for good behavior.

The ultimate goal for believers is to give each child a lifelong passion for following Christ, not simply high marks for good behavior.

How can you encourage your son to connect with Christ instead of a rulebook?

How are you modeling a passion for following Christ to your son?

WRAP UP

• • •

PRAY TOGETHER, asking the Lord to help you be motivated to parent with His love this week.

Lord, give us wisdom as we guide our sons this week. Guide us as we love them and teach them more about You. Help us live our lives as positive examples of what it means to follow You and live for Your glory. Amen.

● **READ AND COMPLETE** the activities for this section before your next group time. For further insight, read chapter 1 from the book *Bringing Up Boys.*

As parents, you perform two roles simultaneously: playing offense—instilling God-honoring qualities in them—and playing defense—protecting them from immoral and dangerous enticements.

A predictable part of raising boys is their tendency to be risk takers. Boys are often slower to learn from their calamities, blaming "bad luck" for their injuries and assuming their luck will improve on the next try.[1]

Canadian psychologist Barbara Morrongiello studied how boys and girls view risk differently. While females thoroughly consider whether they can get hurt and are less likely to forge ahead if there's a chance of injury, boys will take a chance if they think the danger is worth the risk.[2] Boys may consider that impressing their friends is worth taking a risk. Here's where the "defense" part of parenting is important.

> What examples from culture can you emphasize to counter your son's desire for risk? What examples from your own life experience or from those around him can you use to guide him?

> On the other hand, what are some benefits to a mind-set that recognizes danger as a part of life?

A MALE IDENTITY

You are also to help your son understand how God created him. God designed men and women to be different. We want our sons to embrace their uniqueness and understand their God-given masculinity.

Our culture seeks to redefine male identity, either by downplaying masculinity or by perverting it.

What is a healthy male identity? Our sons are made in the image of God, so their worth is purely in Him. To know how to live as God's man, our boys have the opportunity to look to our perfect example, Jesus.

Jesus was:

- a leader who gave dignity and status to women. (See Luke 13:15-16.)
- completely obedient to God, even when obedience involved risk and unpopularity. (See Phil. 2:8; Luke 13:31-32.)
- aware of when He needed time alone with His Father. (See Mark 1:35; Luke 5:16.)
- in solid relationships with other men who sought to be obedient to God. (See Matt. 26:37; Mark 13:3.)
- moved, saddened, and angered by the state of the fallen world. (See Luke 13:34; John 11:32-36.)
- intentional in helping people in need. (See Matt. 14:13-21.)
- aware that people are sinful, but loved them anyway—even if it meant being painfully honest. (See Mark 8:27-33.)
- against looking at women with lust. (See Matt. 5:27-28.)

Name other qualities Jesus modeled.

Which of the previous qualities do you struggle with?

With God's help, how can you improve in these areas?

Have intentional conversations with your son about these virtues Jesus modeled. Admit your own struggles and let your son share his. Pray together that the Holy Spirit will equip you both to grow to look more like Jesus.

It's possible to promote an environment where it's OK to make mistakes and admit struggles. What effect might that have on your son?

COMBATTING CULTURE

As parents, we must protect our sons from society's definition of a man, which is counter to what Jesus modeled and taught.

What characteristics does our culture attribute to men/consider "manly"?

Where do we get these ideas about men?

It is easy to become numb to the invasion of media and its overt sexuality. You must have open conversations with your son, acknowledging culture's disregard for purity and its pervasive acceptance of lust. As you encourage and model how to properly treat and view women—not as objects, but as images of God—he won't follow society's perception.

● **READ** Psalm 101:3a and Proverbs 23:7a.

How can you guard your son's heart and eyes?

The following are some suggestions to get you thinking.

STEP ONE: KEEP COMPUTERS, TVS, PHONES, AND TABLETS OUT OF BEDROOMS. Keep them in the family room, where you can monitor the screen and the amount of time kids spend on them.

STEP TWO: WATCH SHOWS WITH YOUR SON. Watching together can present teaching situations and dialogue that will help your son make his own right choices.

How will protecting your home from unwholesome shows and games benefit your entire family?

You have an incredible opportunity as a parent to set a solid, healthy example of love, grace, and respect.

How can you better model love, grace, and respect for your son in day-to-day moments?

PERSONAL REFLECTION

• • •

This week, focus on Philippians 4:8: "Finally brothers, whatever is true, whatever is honorable, whatever is just, whatever is pure, whatever is lovely, whatever is commendable—if there is any moral excellence and if there is any praise—dwell on these things."

---

1. Ira Dreyfuss, "Boys and Girls See Risk Differently, Study Says," *Associated Press*, 16 February 1997.
2. Ibid.

WEEK 2
THE **MAGIC**
OF TESTOSTERONE

● **START YOUR GROUP TIME** by discussing what participants discovered in their Reflect homework.

About 100 years ago, explorer Ernest Shackleton supposedly placed an ad in local newspapers that read, "Men wanted for hazardous duty. Small wages. Bitter cold. Long months of complete darkness, constant danger. Safe return doubtful. Honor and recognition in case of success."

According to legend, more than 5,000 men applied, of whom 27 were accepted (and even 1 stowaway made the trip).

What are some reasons men would be drawn to the promises in this ad?

Had the ad been open to both sexes, how many women do you think would have applied? Why?

What would your response be if your son wanted to sign up for guaranteed peril or extreme danger?

● **WATCH CLIP 2** from the study DVD and answer the
following questions:

How would you describe the differences in the male
and female brain?

Testosterone—God's chemical brain rearranger. As the video explains,
boys get a "hormonal bath" in utero. This bath of testosterone
actually damages the brain, altering its structure—particularly
that of the corpus callosum (the nerve fibers that connect the
brain's hemispheres), effectively slowing down the connection and
communication between the left and right sides of the brain.

But which two sections of the brain get bigger and have more
synapses added to them in the hormonal bath? Aggression and sex.

Let's launch into aggression first.

Aggression is linked with risk-taking, which is why, generally speaking,
men tend to be the explorers and conquerors of the unknown.

How can understanding your son's brain development
change the way you relate to him?

CONTINUE YOUR GROUP TIME with this discussion guide.

Men are designed to value change, risk, opportunity, and adventure. And boys are men in training. Their aggressive nature is designed to prepare them for their upcoming roles of provision, protection, and responsibility. Their properly-channeled assertiveness is valuable. The challenge for parents is not to resent or eliminate that excitable nature, but to shape and mold it.

READ 1 Corinthians 11:1.

> Whom do you most often imitate? Whom does your son pattern his life after?

> What would you like to change about the above two answers? How will you make these adjustments?

Kathleen Parker has some excellent advice on molding boys:

> Support them when they're down ... reward good behavior, provide meaningful consequences for unacceptable behavior, make reasonable demands, express moral expectations ... and hug those boys every chance you get. Don't ask them to be men when they're just little boys, but show them how to be real men by demonstrating the thing we as a society seem to have lost: self-control.[1]

READ Galatians 5:22-23.

Choose two fruit and discuss ways to model them to your son this week.

How can you encourage your son to incorporate the fruit of the Spirit in his life, making heart change—not good behavior—the goal?

Our own lack of self-control as parents can crush our sons when they exasperate us to our breaking point. What should we do when we have lost control and said something wounding? Repair the damage as quickly as possible. In golf, when you make a divot, the faster you get that tuft of grass back in place, the faster its roots reconnect. The same applies to relating to our sons. Apologize and seek to reconcile right away, giving them a godly example of what to do when they make mistakes. Remember: you're not modeling perfection; you are modeling authenticity and reliance on God.

READ Mark 2:17.

What is your son learning from your example?

SEX

Today's moral relativism has confused the distinctions between right and wrong, proper and improper, and priceless and worthless. Boys, with their tendencies to push the limits and defy authority, are particularly vulnerable to this moral free fall, succumbing to the idea that their abundance of testosterone makes them accountable to no one.

READ 1 Thessalonians 4:3.

> How can you help your son learn to have self-control over his body and mind?

READ Colossians 3:5.

Remind your sons repeatedly and emphatically of the biblical teaching about sexual immorality. Explain that someone who violates those laws not only hurts himself, but also wounds the girl and cheats the man she will eventually marry. Tell your sons not to take anything that doesn't belong to them—especially the moral purity of a woman.

We must counterbalance the messages of our culture, pointing out the consequences of living in contradiction to the laws of God.

> What are some ways you can offset the messages of sexual immorality from our culture—from movies, advertisements, the Internet, and so forth?

THIS WEEK'S INSIGHTS

• • •

- The challenge for parents is not to resent or eliminate boys' excitable nature, but to shape and mold it.
- When you say something wounding, apologize and seek to reconcile, showing what men do when they make mistakes.
- Tell your son that sexual immorality hurts him, the woman he has sex with, and her future spouse.

READ 1 Corinthians 6:18 and 1 Thessalonians 4:6.

According to these verses, who receives the consequences of sexual immorality?

Begin these conversations early, geared to the age and maturity of your son.

How can you create an environment that promotes open, respectful discussion about purity and sex?

WRAP UP

• • •

PRAY TOGETHER, as you prepare to have a conversation about sex with your son and when best to start the discussion.

Lord, give us the wisdom and discernment as we discuss this topic with our sons. Help us to clearly explain how You designed sex as a gift. We pray that You would help our sons understand the value of living a pure life that honors You through obedience. Amen.

● **READ AND COMPLETE** the activities for this section before your next group time. For further insight, read chapter 14 from the book *Bringing Up Boys.*

The American Academy of Pediatrics conducted a study that showed the average child is subjected to 14,000 sexual references on television a year.[2] And that's just television, not the Internet. One of your most important assignments as a parent is to preserve the mental and physical health of your son. You wouldn't think of letting someone injure him physically if you could prevent it. In the same way, we must protect our sons from the unwholesome messages from the media.

We must prayerfully ask the Lord to supply us with what we need to shepherd our kids safely through the minefields of an increasingly sinful society. Everything we do during these foundational years should be bathed in prayer. Stay connected to Jesus as a parent, seeking His wisdom as you engage your son in conversations about purity and sex.

● **READ** 1 Thessalonians 4:7-8.

UNDERSTANDING PORN

Let's start with society's biggest deterrent to sex the way God designed it: porn. Porn is the prime thief of sexual enjoyment (Who can measure up to a fantasy?) and romance (Porn teaches you arousal and release, not commitment and tenderness.). Be shrewd yourself and teach your son to protect himself against tempting situations.

God designed sex to consummate a union—to make two into one flesh—so He designed the following four hormones to be present in sexual activity:

1. **DOPAMINE,** the reward hormone—causes us to ignore negatives and focus on feelings of ecstasy and arousal.

2. **NOREPINEPHRINE**—takes whatever you are experiencing and sears it in your brain.
3. **OXYTOCIN,** the cuddle hormone—causes you to bond with whatever or whoever you are with.
4. **SEROTONIN**—creates a sense of calmness and release from stress.

These chemicals are great when you are experiencing intimacy with your spouse, but when you're flooding your brain with reward chemicals while viewing porn, you are limiting your ability to connect sexually with a *real person* since you are associating all these fantastic feelings with a picture or film.[3]

And you're not just bonding; you're becoming addicted. Addiction hijacks the brain's reward and motivation circuitry, making "normal pleasures lose their appeal [until] the only thing that matters is the drug." An addiction is defined by

- a craving/preoccupation for the substance.
- an inability to stop.
- progressive use of the substance in spite of negative consequences.[4]

Why do men continue using porn in spite of negative consequences? Because "they have adopted viewing and acting out to pornography as a way of dealing with stress, venting their frustration or feelings of helplessness, or salving their feelings of depression and insecurity." Porn pushes away reality. And reality hurts.[5]

How do you deal with stress?

How do you care for yourself when you feel helpless, frustrated, or insecure?

How are you modeling and explaining these coping mechanisms to your son?

This is life-altering stuff: either you show your boys how to handle life's ongoing struggles or they learn to cope from their friends and culture, who don't have their best interests at heart. You need to train them in the toughest battlefield—their minds when they feel weak.

READ 1 Corinthians 10:13.

In what ways have your life experiences prepared you to help your son learn how to succeed when facing his own struggles?

How can you encourage your son's adventurous nature while teaching him to resist temptation?

Teach your son your healthy coping mechanisms. Show your son how to handle stress and temptation and whom he can run to for shelter.

UNDERSTANDING AGGRESSION

The aggressive nature in boys is designed for a purpose; it prepares them for the "provision and protection" roles they inhabit later in life. Properly channeled, it becomes a helpful assertiveness.

But often, instead of the aggressiveness being shaped and civilized by parents, it can be exacerbated by their disengagement. Many parents are simply too busy and distracted or too immature and selfish to meet the pressing needs of their sons. Our job as parents is to engage them and train them in kindness and respect. Children love justice and they're very uneasy in a world of injustice and abuse. Therefore, when we connect with them and insist on civility in our homes, we're laying a foundation for human kindness in the world of adulthood to come.

Start civility training with your words.

● **READ** James 3:6,8.

Most often, we unleash the poison of our tongues when we are angry. Our "fight or flight" mechanism is an involuntary reaction. What is voluntary is our choice of response in that heated moment. We can learn to take a step back, hold our tongues, and remove ourselves from provoking situations.

> Think of a time you were angry recently. How did you act in your anger? What happened? What could you have done differently?

> What's the difference between reacting and responding?

> What other techniques could you use the next time you find yourself becoming angry?

> In what ways could you be more consistent in your tone of voice with your son?

> How will these methods benefit him?

● **READ** Matthew 15:18 and Ezekiel 11:19-20a.

What do these verses teach us about the source of our anger and what we can do about it?

PERSONAL REFLECTION
• • •

Outline what you will say in a talk with your son about sex and aggression:

What are positive expressions of them?

What are negative expressions of them?

Help him identify what is healthy and unhealthy, so he has a clear understanding of the best choices he can make.

1. Kathleen Parker, "Let's Give Our Boys a Gift: Self-Control," *USA Today*, 15 September 1999, 17 (A).
2. Steve Rubenstein, "Doctors Advise TV Blackout for Little Kids," *San Francisco Chronicle*, 4 August 1999, [cited 3 July 2014]. Available from the Internet: *http://www.sfgate.com/health/article/Doctors-Advise-TV-Blackout-For-Little-Kids-2914810.php*.
3. See articles under "Sexual Addiction" on *candeobehaviorchange.com,* [cited 16 October 2013]. Available from the Internet: *http://candeobehaviorchange.com*.
4. William M. Struthers, "Porn Addiction in the Brain," *Enrichment Journal*, [cited 16 October 2013]. Available from the Internet: *http://enrichmentjournal.ag.org/201103/201103_080_porn_addict.cfm*.
5. Ibid.

AN IMPROVED VIEW OF
VIEW OF
MASCULINITY

● **START YOUR GROUP TIME** by discussing what participants discovered in their Reflect homework.

In the words of psychologist Robert Stoller, "Masculinity is an achievement."[1] It requires societal and parental support.

But from the 1970s even through the late '80s, parents and society were under the impression that boys needed to be fixed—to be less masculine, a trait that was, supposedly, only a byproduct of a biased patriarchal culture.

What does masculinity mean to you?

From the Latin *masculus,* "masculine" carries the meaning of "male, masculine; worthy of a man," or "having the appropriate qualities of the male sex, manly, virile, powerful."

When you hear the words "manly, male, virile," do you have a positive or negative reaction? Why?

How would you define "positive" masculinity?

"Negative" masculinity?

WATCH CLIP 3 from the study DVD and answer the following questions:

One particular pitfall caused by the movement to make the sexes equal is the fear of respecting and even enjoying the well-designed differences between males and females.

What does a healthy appreciation of the differences between the sexes look like?

What does an unhealthy assessment look like?

How can you encourage your son to embrace his masculinity?

How can you encourage your son to respect women?

● **CONTINUE YOUR GROUP TIME** with this discussion guide.

In "hidden picture" games, kids look for specific items (a teacup, a wrench, a clock, etc.) that have been drawn to blend into the illustration. Similarly, our culture plays a hidden picture game with our children, obscuring lies about their God-given traits. Yet Scripture reveals to us authentic masculinity. As parents, we must be intentional to teach our boys to recognize and act on biblical truth.

● **READ** Genesis 1:27,31a.

God made man and woman in His image.

God created male and female.

God called His creation good.

> You are created in the image of God. What's so special about that?

> God created two sexes. What's so great about being male or female?

> You, as a man or woman, are deemed a "good" creation by the Creator. What does that mean to you?

The beauty, the mystery, the nobility of being male and female has been traded for the idea that the sexes are identical except for their reproductive apparatus. "Unisex" is supposedly the word of the enlightened. But denying the differences does not replace truth.

The sexes obstinately continue in their dissimilarities. Let's take a moment to enjoy them.

Moms, what do you like about being female?

What are some qualities or abilities of men you admire?

What unique qualities of women do you wish men would value and respect more often?

Dads, what do you like about being male?

What are some qualities or abilities of women that you admire?

What unique qualities of men do you wish women would value and respect more often?

How will you pass each of these values to your son?

You, the parent, have an important role to play. In this new era, masculinity is taught as a good and healthy characteristic of men. Masculinity involves moral character, self-control, integrity, confidence, and obedience to a God who created men and sent His Son to save His creation.

Let's consider some verses from Scripture to help us maintain a healthy outlook on masculinity.

● **READ** Romans 12:2.

> Why start our re-education in masculinity by focusing on our thoughts?

Martin Luther once told the story of a young man admitting his lust for women to a hermit. The old hermit replied, "You cannot prevent the birds from flying over your head. But let them only fly and do not let them build a nest in the hair of your head. Let them be thoughts and remain such; but do not let them become conclusions."[2]

Though we may have fleeting negative thoughts of males and females, we have an obligation to refuse them a permanent residence in our minds. But this task takes the work of the Spirit and our awareness.

> How do you treat the opposite sex relationships in your life, particularly your son's mother/father?

THIS WEEK'S INSIGHTS

• • •

- God created male and female and called them "good."
- Discard negative thoughts about the opposite sex.
- Watch what you put before your eyes—does it uplift or demean the opposite sex?

READ Job 31:1.

What happens when we harbor negative or ungodly thoughts about the opposite sex?

READ Psalm 101:3.

If your television/Internet/book choices do not esteem men and women, what are you communicating to your son?

WRAP UP

• • •

PRAY TOGETHER, asking the Lord to provide healthy examples of masculinity and femininity based on biblical truth.

> Lord, we know that You intentionally designed
> men and women differently so that we may
> complement one another for Your glory. Help us
> to portray a healthy example of our God-given
> roles as we raise our sons. We pray that he learns
> to live according to Your Word as he wrestles with
> the overwhelming influence of culture. Amen.

READ AND COMPLETE the activities for this section before your next group time. For further insight, read chapters 2 and 9 from *Bringing Up Boys*.

Sons are emotionally attached to their moms until about 18 months of age. Then they begin to dis-identify with their moms and identify with their dads.[3] At about 3 to 5 years of age, boys crave the involvement of their fathers and try to emulate their behavior and mannerisms. In light of this, fathers need to mirror and affirm their son's maleness, showing him the three As: his affection, attention, and approval.[4] However, Harvard researchers found that 91 percent of men who recalled no maternal closeness developed coronary disease, hypertension, and alcoholism by their midlife years.[5] What does all the scientific research prove? Both moms and dads play essential roles in the development of their sons.

What was your relationship with your mother and father like?

What memories and values from your own parents do you want to cultivate with your son? What experiences do you hope to improve upon?

READ Luke 3:21-22.

How did God exemplify the three A's in these verses?

READ Luke 15:11-32.

How did the father demonstrate the three A's to his sons in this passage?

In what ways can moms and dads intentionally show the three A's at each stage of their child's development?

Why do your sons and our society desperately need men to model masculinity with your sons? Sociologist Peter Karl explains that because boys spend up to 80 percent of their time with women, they don't know how to act as men when they grow up, directly affecting the relationship between the sexes. Men become helpless and more like big kids.[6]

Dr. Michael Gurian said it this way: "Every time you raise a loving, wise, and responsible man, you have created a better world for women. Women [today] are having to bond to half-men, with boys who were not fully raised to manhood, don't know how to bond, don't know what their responsibilities are to humanity, and don't have a strong sense of service."[7] Today's fathers can change that.

Masculinity is the fruit of an encouraging family and society that values the gift of men. Without it, a boy has no sense of belonging, identity, affirmation, or intimacy.

Boys need to have masculinity defined for them biblically. Otherwise the culture will distort the definition.

What does the culture say a man should be?

● **READ** 1 Kings 2:1-3.

What do these verses reveal a man should be?

STRUCTURE FOR MASCULINITY

Boys need structure, they need supervision, and they need to be civilized. When raised in a laissez-faire environment that is devoid of guidance and leadership in masculinity, they challenge social conventions and common sense—further derailing them from the tracks of manhood and putting them on the trails of half-men.

The beginning of structure is love. As Josh McDowell says, "Rules without relationship lead to rebellion."[8] Just laying down the law will create a spirit of defiance in them, so engage your sons, play games and sports with them, and build bridges by having fun as a family.

Relationships are built with regular contact. The presence of parents is very beneficial at four key times of the day: early morning, after school, dinnertime, and bedtime. When that regular contact is combined with other shared activities between parents and kids, sons feel a sense of connection with their family, deterring them from harmful behavior.[9]

> How often are you present at those key times each day?
> How can you change your schedule to be present more?

Love is inherent in discipline. Many parents are afraid to show displeasure to kids for fear of wounding or rejecting them. On the contrary, sons need to know who is in charge and that they are safe in that person's care. If you are afraid to make your son uncomfortable or unhappy when he misbehaves, he will sense your tentativeness and push you farther, resulting in ineffectual, irritated parents and rebellious, lost children.

● **READ** Hebrews 12:5b-6.

> How are you loving your son when you discipline him?

What is your current plan of discipline when your son misbehaves? What's working well? What isn't?

Take time to build the consistent discipline structure your son needs. Making a plan will keep you from acting out of anger and frustration.

Structured masculinity also involves the civilization of men. You are the instructors for this civilization, training your son in basic manners and life skills, including how to:

While it's great to have your son behave well, keep your eyes on his heart.

- shake hands/make introductions
- behave admirably at the table
- show respect to women, men, children, and animals
- apply for jobs
- speak/text/post respectfully
- keep a tidy living space
- be punctual
- be a team player
- apologize without excusing behavior or blaming others
- lose honorably
- tithe, save, and invest
- control his temper
- resist temptation
- stand up for what he believes in

The above list is not meant to train your son to perform while harboring a heart that chafes at your behavioral demands. The above courtesies need to come from a heart that recognizes the image of God in others and desires to respect that image and care for others—not just put on a good show.

How can you encourage these traits in your son?

What's the difference between merely following commands and choosing obedience?

ESTABLISHING RITES OF PASSAGE

Rites of passage also help boys engage with the elusive sense of conquest and camaraderie that's part of masculinity. In America, we tend to identify rites such as graduating, getting a job, getting married, and having kids. But there's a benefit to identifying rites for not only becoming adults, but adult males. Sometimes, initiations are helpful in proving prowess, encouraging boys to feel like extraordinary men

For example, in one boys camp, male campers are offered the chance to become Chiefs if, in one night, they finish a ropes course, make a roaring fire last six hours (with only one match), do a one-mile run, then finish the last three hours without speaking. Few succeed. While a rite of passage doesn't have to be that elaborate, the recognition is no less important.

> What value is found in celebrating your son's
> accomplishments toward becoming a man?

PERSONAL REFLECTION
● ● ●

Brainstorm and plan a rite of passage—a time of training and then testing, followed by a ceremony that marks the occasion. For more ceremony ideas, try *Raising a Modern Day Knight* by Robert Lewis, which defines manhood as rejecting passivity, accepting responsibility, leading courageously, and expecting the greater reward.

1. I. Bieber et al., *Homosexuality: A Psychoanalytic Study of Male Homosexuals* (New York: Basic Books, 1982).
2. Eric Gritsch, *The Wit of Martin Luther* (Minneapolis: Augsburg Fortress, 2006), 53.
3. Joseph Nicolosi, *Preventing Homosexuality: A Parent's Guide,* chapter 1.
4. Ibid, chapter 3.
5. "Parent's Love Affects Child's Health," *Reuters,* 10 March 1997.
6. Hannah C. Berlin, "Lads Night Out Can Save Your Marriage," *London Daily Express,* 25 April 2000.
7. Michael Gurian, *The Wonder of Boys* (New York: Jeremy Tarcher/Putna, 1996).
8. Josh McDowell, "Helping Your Kids to Say No," *Focus on the Family,* 16 October 1987.
9. Michael D. Resnick et al., "Protecting Adolescents from harm: Findings from the National Longitudinal Study on Adolescent Health," *Journal of the American Medical Association,* 10 September 1999.

WEEK 4 THE **IMPORTANCE** OF BULL ELEPHANTS

● **START YOUR GROUP TIME** by discussing what participants discovered in their Reflect homework.

Several years ago in Georgia, the Bulldogs of Rockdale County High School overcame a big deficit to win the state basketball championship. Coach Cleveland Stroud was so proud of his team. But a few days later, while watching a film of the game, he noticed an ineligible player on the court for forty-five seconds.

He called the Georgia High School Association and reported the violation, costing the school the title and the trophy.

When asked about it at a press conference, Coach Stroud said, "Some people have said we should have kept quiet about it. That it was just forty-five seconds, and that the player wasn't really an impact player. But you gotta do what's honest and right. I told my team that people forget the scores of basketball games. They don't ever forget what you're made out of."[1]

You can be certain that every member of the Bulldogs' team will remember the character of Coach Stroud. A letter to the editor of the local newspaper said, "We have scandals in Washington and cheating on Wall Street. Thank goodness we live in Rockdale County, where honor and integrity are alive and being practiced."[2]

What qualities are you modeling for your son?

When has he seen you exemplify a specific positive quality even when it was inconvenient to do so?

● **WATCH CLIP 4** from the study DVD and answer the following questions:

Boys aren't born knowing how to be men.

> Do you believe that statement? If so, what kind of man do you hope your son becomes? (list qualities)

> Which of those qualities do you most struggle with?

When I was headed in the wrong direction, my mother called the "bull elephant" home. She phoned my father and said, "I need you." My father caught a train home and canceled his revival career for the next four years—a huge sacrifice.

> Why did my father make that sacrifice?

> Who benefited from that sacrifice? How?

● **CONTINUE YOUR GROUP TIME** with this discussion guide.

Because boys watch their parents intently, your demeanor and actions are far more efficient at training sons than lecturing, scolding, punishing, bribing, and cajoling.

If you blow up regularly and insult your spouse, your boys will learn to treat others disrespectfully. If you curse or manipulate people or fight with your coworkers, your boys will probably follow suit. If you are selfish or mean or angry, you'll see those characteristics displayed in the next generation.

The opposite is also true. If you are honest, trustworthy, caring, loving, self-disciplined, and God-fearing, your boys will be shaped by those traits. If you are deeply committed to Jesus Christ and live by biblical principles, your children will probably follow in your footsteps. So much depends on what they observe in parents, for better or worse.

What are some negative traits your parents displayed?

Which of those traits do you see in yourself?

What are some positive traits your parents displayed?

Which of those traits do you see in yourself?

Children may not remember what you say, but they are usually impacted for life by what you do.

What do you value?

During each day, what takes up sizable quantities of your time?

In your wallet, what takes out sizable amounts of cash?

In your mind, what takes up sizable amounts of reflection and pondering?

How do these things benefit your son?

If you had a difficult time thinking of benefits, what are some adjustments that can be made to each area?

What should our framework be for pleasing the Lord with our time, money, and thoughts? Jesus summed it up nicely.

● **READ** Matthew 22:37-38.

How does one love well? Let's seek Scripture again.

● **READ** 1 Corinthians 13:4-7.

List the qualities below:

Love is/does	Love is not/does not

We, too, are following an example—the one God sets for us. If "God is love" (1 John 4:8), then He is patient, kind, rejoicing in truth, hoping, enduring, and so on. We are not perfect models for our sons, but we can direct them to the Source of that perfect love, letting them know how we all are flawed and in continual need of that love from God.

Remember the importance of the presence of a father in the life of his son. Keep in mind that a son needs his father to be present as often as possible to model himself on him and his walk with God. If there's no bull elephant around, there's nothing to model himself on, except what the culture and his friends offer.

If you are a single mom, I realize that your challenges are unique. You have a difficult scale to balance—loving your son well and launching him into manhood. Ask the Lord to help you find godly male role models to offer what you cannot provide. Involve your son in the church youth group, sports teams, and groups like Young Life. He needs these chances to interact with mature Christian leaders.

Who can become a godly example if your son's father and/or grandfather is/are absent?

THIS WEEK'S INSIGHTS

• • •

- Sons tend to model themselves not after their parents' sermons but their parents' lives.
- What do your time, money, and thoughts show to be the desires of your heart?
- Be present for your son to model himself after you.

In the last two weeks, how many times did you spend five minutes or more with your son?

Was anything electronic on during those times?

Did he have your full attention? Did you have his?

WRAP UP

• • •

PRAY TOGETHER, asking the Lord to help you live your life as a godly example for your son. Pray also for others who influence your son on a regular basis.

> Lord, we pray that as we live out each day, we would be godly examples in our words, actions, and attitudes. Help us to model what it means to be a godly person who follows You each and every day. We pray also for others in our sons' lives, that they would point to You rather than distract our sons from biblical truth. Amen.

READ AND COMPLETE the activities for this section before your next group time. For further insight, read chapter 15 from the book *Bringing Up Boys*.

> Where can dads find a good role model of a family man? Brainstorm some sources to check out.

HOW TO BE A BULL ELEPHANT

The following four roles have been ridiculed and attacked by the media. As a result, many fathers have a poor concept of what they are supposed to do or how to get it done. But men were designed to take care of the people they love, even if it involves personal sacrifice. When they fulfill that responsibility, their wives and children usually live in greater peace and harmony.

1. SERVE AS THE FAMILY PROVIDER. Even though the majority of wives and moms work outside the home, it is still a man's charge to assure that the financial needs of the family are met.

READ 1 Timothy 5:8.

Some men hold good jobs but remain immature. Their willingness to work must be combined with a devotion to a cause, to something greater than themselves. Those two traits—the ability to live responsibly and have a sense of mission—help our boys overcome their self-centeredness and begin to see themselves as men. As parents, then, our job is to teach kids to work and introduce them to the meaning associated with it—providing for and protecting their families.

Beyond financially, how is a father a provider for his family?

2. SERVE AS THE LEADER OF THE CLAN. Husbands are to love their wives to the point of sacrificing themselves for their spouses.

● **READ** Ephesians 5:25.

How did Christ love the church? He gave up His life for her. Fathers are called to lead by example, lovingly and unselfishly remaining devoted to his wife and her well-being.

How can fathers serve as the leaders of their family, setting an example for their sons?

3. SERVE AS PROTECTOR. He is to shield his family members from the outside world and yet teach them how to cope with it successfully. He is the one family members come to when they feel threatened. He defends their honor and sees that the house is safe at night and kids are home at a reasonable time.

How can fathers serve as the protector of their households, setting an example for their sons?

4. PROVIDE SPIRITUAL DIRECTION AT HOME. Read Scripture to your son. Read the adventure stories and the love stories. Explain the difference between right and wrong. Set the example of going to church, serving others, and tithing as part of life. The most important of all parental responsibilities is to teach them who they are as children of God and what they have been placed here to do.

READ Deuteronomy 6:4-9.

> How can a father serve as the spiritual director of his home, setting an example for his son?

Consider how Jesus Christ led men when He was on earth—with compassion, confrontation, and with a great story.

> Take a moment to summarize your life story thus far. Start with what you live for. (Look back to the Engage section on what you spend your time, money, and thoughts on.)

> Now fill in the blank: "As a kid, I grew up seeking _____ (what you live for)."

> If you achieved what you were seeking as a child, how does it make you feel? If you didn't achieve that goal, how does it affect you now?

Maybe your story is one of materialism. Boy grows up wanting success. Boy finds success (defined by having a large house and a nice car). Success makes him feel ... well, how does it make you feel?

> How engaging is your story? Does it ignite your passions? Make you grow? Bring joy? If not, what do you want to change?

How engaging is your story to your son?

You don't have to build an orphanage in Burundi … or maybe, you
might. You don't have to serve at a weekly luncheon for the homeless
… or maybe, you might. Think long-term: what effect would trying
a new story have on you, your son, and your family's story? Maybe
yours is the generation that changes the tide.

Think of some wild, even outrageous ideas to kick
your story into overdrive.

List some less outrageous, but doable "wildness" that
could alter your story.

What if you prayed for a story that drives you and your
family closer to God? Is that scary?

● **READ** Matthew 15:8.

You may discover that neither you nor your son are ignited by that
life story. But don't live with regret; instead, consider something new
and refreshing.

Now pick one doable, wild thing you can do with your
family this month. Put it on your calendar. Present it
to the family. Up the ante of your story.

Give your son a story he can be inspired by. He may not like it at first, but I encourage you to keep trying.

PERSONAL REFLECTION
• • •

In the end, your story will illustrate what you think about Jesus and whether He is the Source of your life. As a human, you will fail. Do not aim for perfection; aim for connection with God's Spirit and internal honesty—honesty in your faith, your failures, and your ongoing faults.

Kids are experts at noticing inconsistencies between what parents say and do. Be the parent who admits your errors. Let your son see the process you go through when you choose poorly—how to recognize it, reveal it, and make reparations for it. And let that be a blessing to you both.

1. William E. Schmidt, "For Town and Team, Honor Is Its Own Reward," *New York Times*, 22 May 1987, [cited 3 July 2014]. Available from the Internet: *http://www.nytimes.com/1987/05/25/us/for-town-and-team-honor-is-its-own-reward.html*.
2. Ibid.

Key Insights

WEEK 1

- Boys are made in the image of our adventurous God.
- Boys need instruction that builds them up according to their needs.
- Our goal as parents is to give our sons a lifelong passion for Christ, not simply high marks for good behavior.

WEEK 2

- The challenge for parents is not to resent or eliminate boys' excitable nature, but to shape, and mold it.
- When you say something wounding, apologize and seek to reconcile, showing what men do when they make mistakes.
- Tell your son that sexual immorality hurts him, the woman he has sex with, and her future spouse.

WEEK 3

- God created male and female and called them "good."
- Discard negative thoughts about the opposite sex.
- Watch what you put before your eyes—does it uplift or demean the opposite sex?

WEEK 4

- Sons tend to model themselves not after their parents' sermons but their parents' lives.
- What do your time, money, and thoughts show to be the desires of your heart?
- Be present for your son to model himself after you.

Leader Notes

It's time for a leadership adventure. Don't worry; you don't have to have all the answers. Your role is to facilitate the group discussion, getting participants back on topic when they stray, encouraging everyone to share honestly and authentically, and guiding those who might dominate the conversation to make sure others are also getting some time to share.

As facilitator, take time to look over this entire study guide, noting the order and requirements of each session. Watch all the videos as well. Take time to read the suggested chapters (noted in the beginning of each Reflect section) from the book *Bringing Up Boys* (ISBN 978-1-4143-9133-5). And pray over the material, the prospective participants, and your time together.

You have the option of extending your group's study by showing the films *Bringing Up Boys* and *Your Legacy*. You can also keep it to four weeks by using just this study guide and DVD. The study is easy to customize for your group's needs.

Go over the How to Use This Study and the Guidelines for Groups sections with participants, making everyone aware of best practices and the steps of each session. Then dive into Week 1.

In establishing a schedule for each group meeting, consider ordering these elements for the hour of time together:

1. Connect—10 minutes
2. Watch—15 minutes
3. Engage—35 minutes

Be sure to allow time during each session to show the video clip. All four clips are approximately eight minutes or less in length. Reflect refers to the home study or activities done between group sessions.

Beginning with session 2, encourage some sharing regarding the previous week's Reflect home study. Usually at least one Connect question allows for this interaction. Sharing about the previous week's activities encourages participants to study on their own and be ready to share with their group during the next session.

As the study comes to a close, consider some ways to keep in touch. There may be some additional studies for which group members would like information. Some may be interested in knowing more about your church.

Occasionally, a group member may have needs that fall outside the realm of a supportive small group. If someone would be better served by the pastoral staff at your church or a professional counselor, please maintain a list of professionals to privately offer to that person, placing his/her road to recovery in the hands of a qualified pastor or counselor.

Use the space below to make notes or to identify specific page numbers and questions you would like to discuss with your small group each week based on their needs and season of life.

Further Resources

Need more guidance? Check out the following for help.

ON PARENTING:

The New Dare to Discipline by Dr. James Dobson

The New Strong-Willed Child by Dr. James Dobson

Bringing Up Boys by Dr. James Dobson

Bringing Up Girls by Dr. James Dobson

Dr. Dobson's Handbook of Family Advice by Dr. James Dobson

Night Light for Parents by Dr. James Dobson

Parenting Isn't for Cowards by Dr. James Dobson

Temper Your Child's Tantrums by Dr. James Dobson

Raising Boys and Girls by Sissy Goff, David Thomas, and Melissa Trevathan

Love No Matter What by Brenda Garrison

Intentional Parenting by Sissy Goff, David Thomas, and Melissa Trevathan

The Back Door to Your Teen's Heart by Melissa Trevathan

5 Love Languages by Gary Chapman

5 Conversations You Must Have with Your Daughter by Vicki Courtney

Parenting Teens magazine

HomeLife magazine

ParentLife magazine

The Parent Adventure by Selma and Rodney Wilson

Experiencing God at Home by Richard Blackaby and Tom Blackaby

Love Dare for Parents by Stephen Kendrick and Alex Kendrick

Authentic Parenting in a Postmodern Culture by Mary E. DeMuth

Grace-Based Parenting by Tim Kimmel

ON DISCUSSING FAITH WITH YOUR BOYS:

Bringing the Gospel Home by Randy Newman

Firsthand by Ryan Shook and Josh Shook

God Distorted by John Bishop

Sticky Faith by Dr. Kara E. Powell and Dr. Chap Clark

Parenting Beyond Your Capacity by Reggie Joiner and Carey Nieuwhof

A Praying Life by Paul Miller

Faith Conversations for Families by Jim Burns

Introducing Your Child to Christ

Your most significant calling and privilege as a parent is to introduce your children to Jesus Christ. A good way to begin this conversation is to tell them about your own faith journey.

Outlined below is a simple gospel presentation you can share with your child. Define any terms they don't understand and make it more conversational, letting the Spirit guide your words and allowing your child to ask questions and contribute along the way.

GOD RULES. The Bible tells us God created everything, and He's in charge of everything. (See Gen. 1:1; Rev. 4:11; Col. 1:16-17.)

WE SINNED. We all choose to disobey God. The Bible calls this sin. Sin separates us from God and deserves God's punishment of death. (See Rom. 3:23; 6:23.)

GOD PROVIDED. God sent Jesus, the perfect solution to our sin problem, to rescue us from the punishment we deserve. It's something we, as sinners, could never earn on our own. Jesus alone saves us. (See John 3:16; Eph. 2:8-9.)

JESUS GIVES. He lived a perfect life, died on the cross for our sins, and rose again. Because Jesus gave up His life for us, we can be welcomed into God's family for eternity. This is the best gift ever! (See Rom. 5:8; 2 Cor. 5:21; 1 Pet. 3:18; Eph. 2:8-9.)

WE RESPOND. Believe in your heart that Jesus alone saves you through what He's already done on the cross. Repent, by turning away from your sin. Tell God and others that your faith is in Jesus. (See John 14:6; Rom. 10:9-10,13.)

If your child is ready to respond, explain what it means for Jesus to be Lord of their life. Guide them to a time in prayer to repent and express their belief in Jesus. If your child responds in faith, celebrate! You now have the opportunity to disciple them to be more like Christ.

BUILD YOUR FAMILY LEGACY.

Dr. James Dobson leads you through his classic messages and new insights for today's families in these eight DVD-based Bible studies. Each Building a Family Legacy Bible study includes four-sessions with personal reflection and discussion guides along with a DVD of Dr. Dobson's teachings, introduced by his son, Ryan. Studies include:

Your Legacy Bible Study
Bringing Up Boys Bible Study
Bringing Up Girls Bible Study
Dare to Discipline Bible Study
The Strong-Willed Child Bible Study
Straight Talk to Men Bible Study
Love for a Lifetime Bible Study
Wanting to Believe Bible Study

Learn more at LifeWay.com/Legacy

DR. JAMES DOBSON **BUILDING A FAMILY LEGACY**™

Dr. James Dobson's **BUILDING A FAMILY LEGACY** campaign includes films, Bible studies, and books designed to help families of all ages and stages. Dr. Dobson's wisdom, insight, and humor promise to strengthen marriages and help parents meet the remarkable challenges of raising children. Most importantly, **BUILDING A FAMILY LEGACY** will inspire parents to lead their children to personal faith in Jesus Christ.

Learn more at

BUILDINGAFAMILYLEGACY.COM

BUILDING A FAMILY LEGACY BOOKS

From Dr. James Dobson and Tyndale Momentum

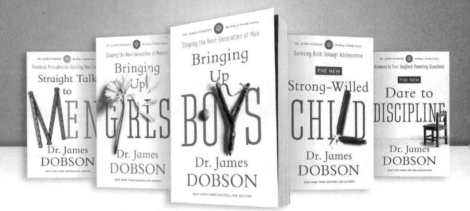

BRINGING UP BOYS • 978-1-4143-9133-5
Also available in hardcover (978-0-8423-5266-6) and audio CDs
(978-0-8423-2297-3)

BRINGING UP GIRLS • 978-1-4143-9132-8
Also available in hardcover (978-1-4143-0127-3) and audio CDs
read by Dr. James Dobson (978-1-4143-3650-3)

THE NEW STRONG-WILLED CHILD • 978-1-4143-9134-2
Also available in hardcover (978-0-8423-3622-2) and audio
CDs (978-0-8423-8799-6), as well as *The New Strong-Willed
Child Workbook* (978-1-4143-0382-6)

THE NEW DARE TO DISCIPLINE • 978-1-4143-9135-9

STRAIGHT TALK TO MEN • 978-1-4143-9131-1

AVAILABLE IN 2015

LOVE FOR A LIFETIME
Revised and expanded edition
978-1-4964-0328-5